Fear Not

Thoughts on Living in Today's World

Pope John Paul II

Edited by Alexandria Hatcher

A Giniger Book

Andrews McMeel Publishing

Kansas City

www.andrewsmcmeel.com

99 01 02 03 RDC 10 9 8 7 6 5 4 3 2 1

Library of Congress Cataloging-in-Publication Data
John Paul II, Pope, 1920–
    Fear not : thoughts on living in today's world / Pope John Paul II ; edited by Alexandria Hatcher.
        p.   cm.
    Includes bibliographical references (p.   ).
    ISBN 0-8362-8290-6 (hc.)
    1. Christian life—Catholic authors. 2. Christian life—Quotations, maxims, etc. I. Hatcher, Alexandria. II. Title.
BX2350.2.J635   1999
248.482—dc21
                                                                98-36498
                                                                CIP

Contents

Introduction

In a world of violence and threatened families, some see Pope John Paul II as a voice in a modern wilderness. He stands firm against the "profound change in the way in which life and relationships between people are considered."[1]

In the face of daily fears, he warns that "serious demographic, social and family problems which weigh upon many of the world's peoples and which require responsible and effective attention . . . are left open to false and deceptive solutions, opposed to the truth and the good of persons and nations."[2]

Today, "conscience itself . . . is finding it increasingly difficult to distinguish between good and evil in what concerns the basic value of human life."[3]

He asks us to "work to ensure that justice and solidarity will increase and that a new culture of human life will be affirmed, for the building of an authentic civilization of truth and love."[4]

1

The Holy Father's thoughts herein focus on our primary relationships: to the self, to others, and to God. Included are two brief interludes: on the Holy Spirit who guides us, and on the spirituality of work, where we manifest connections to all relationships.

Alexandria Hatcher

Relating
to
Oneself

Do not be afraid to be holy.[5]

There is need to be humble so that divine grace may operate in us, transform our lives and bring out fruits of goodness.

*T*he apostolic tradition of the Church
as *a living reality* and not merely as
a relic of the past becomes a conscious part
of your vision of faith.

*B*ut why is man afraid?
Perhaps exactly because, in consequence
of this negation [of God] of his,
he remains alone in the last analysis,
metaphysically alone . . . interiorly alone.

The ultimate foundation
of the value and dignity of man,
of the meaning of his life,
is the fact that he is
God's image and likeness!

*T*he ultimate reason

why man should live, respect and protect

the life of man *is in God.*

*T*he Christian is in the world
but not of the world. . . . His conduct,
his habits of life, his way of thinking,
of making choices, of evaluating things
and situations . . . happen in the
light of Christ's words,
which are a message of everlasting life.

The Christian ought to live
in the perspective of eternity.

Certainty of the eternal salvation
awaiting us renders the Christian strong
against temptations and patient in tribulations.
"They will harry you," the Divine Master said,
"as they harried me" (Jn 15:20): a great honor.

The Christian is actually called by the Church
to prayer, penitence and fasting,
to interior and exterior shedding of oneself.
He stands before God and recognizes what he is.
He rediscovers himself.

*A*nd the country toward which
we are heading is *the Christian's new life.*
It is a paschal life, which can be realized only
through the "power" and the "grace" of God.

$\mathcal{M}$an must make himself aware that his life runs on in the world between good and evil. Temptation is nothing else but directing toward evil everything which man can and ought to put to good use.

*T*he number and manifold character of our temptations have their basis in that threefold concupiscence of which the First Letter of St. John tells us: "For nothing that the world affords comes from the Father. Carnal allurements, enticement for the eye, and life of empty show— all these are from the world" (1 Jn 2:16).

*I*n St. John's mind, the "world" from which the Christian should keep away is not creation, the work of God which was entrusted to the dominion of man, but the symbol and sign of everything which separates from God, that is, the opposite of "God's kingdom."

Christ does not flatter His hearers.
He does not flatter man with the
semblance of "unrestricted" liberty.
He says, "Know the truth, and the truth
will set you free" (Jn 8:32).
In this way, He shows that liberty was not
given to man only as a gift but also as a duty.

*M*an shall not let [inner] truth be snatched from him under the appearance of "unlimited liberty." . . . He shall not cease to hear the cry of conscience in himself as the cry of Truth, the Truth which surpasses him, . . . which makes him man and decides about his humanity.

The spirit of penitence and the practice of it stimulates us to detach ourselves sincerely from everything superfluous that we have.

*F*ear not to accept Christ in your daily work.

Fear not to accept Him in your "world."

Then this world will be really human.

It will become ever more human.

Only the God-Man can make our

"human world" fully human.

One must accept the call,
one must listen, one must receive,
one must measure one's strength,
and answer, "Yes, yes." Fear not.

*W*e must regain consciousness of sin,
which has become the beginning of every sin on
earth, which has become the lasting foundation
and the source of man's sinfulness.

*T*he struggle between the kingdom of evil,
of the evil spirit, and the Kingdom of God
has not ceased, . . . it is not over. It has only
entered upon a new stage, actually the definitive
stage. In this stage the struggle goes on in ever
new generations of human history.

The consumer attitude does not take all
the truth about man into consideration.
Neither the historical truth, nor the social truth,
nor the interior and the metaphysical truth.
Rather it is a flight from that reality.

Good example does not affect only exterior action but goes deep and builds up the most precious and most active of gifts in the other, namely, adherence to one's own Christian vocation.

At the very center of the mission which Christ received from the Father is found the new man: *the man open to the Father*. The man "open to the Father" means the man who lives in the full dimension of his humanity.

*R*emission of sins supposes knowledge and confession of sins. One and the other signify *the effort to live in truth and love.* It means the action of "the power of truth and love," which forms the new man and transforms the world.

*C*ontradiction is obliteration of the line of demarcation between good and evil, it means calling humanism what is actually "sin."

$\mathcal{D}$early beloved, the truest and most sincere wish I can offer you is only this:

"Turn yourselves into saints,
make yourselves holy soon."

*L*et us be glad to live in these times of ours,
and let us courageously commit ourselves
to the design which Providence is
mysteriously accomplishing.

*T*imes change. . . .
But the fundamental principles,
the sacramental order above all,
remain unchanged.

In baptism we are given a name;
we call it our Christian name.
In the tradition of the Church it is
a saint's name, a name of one of the
heroes among Christ's followers.

*L*et yourselves be led by the hand of the Lord, because he wishes to accomplish Redemption today through your means.

The Redemption is always of today,
because the parable of the good
seed and the weeds is always of today.
The Beatitudes are always of today.

$\mathcal{B}$ut you must prepare yourselves
with a sense of great responsibility and
profound and convinced seriousness.

*B*e serious] in your cultural education,
especially your philosophical, biblical, theological
learning, and in ascetics and discipline,
so as to consecrate yourselves totally and
joyously alone to Jesus and to souls.

"Our inner being is renewed each day"
(2 Cor 4:16).
When God calls, when God converts,
he also gives a mission.

*L*ove the truth before all,
while feeling lively comprehension
of the contemporary society
in which we live.

Gift of the Holy Spirit

Willingness [to accept the Gospel] is, in fact, a manifestation
of grace at work in the soul. "The Spirit blows where it will"
(cf. Jn 3:8). The freedom of the Spirit meets the
freedom of man and fully confirms it.[6]

"As the Father has sent me, so I send you."

He breathed on them and said,

"Receive the Holy Spirit."

Have you received the Holy Spirit?

Have you "accepted" him?

The Spirit acts on each of us differently, in harmony with our individual personality and the characteristics we have inherited from our parents and from the upbringing received in our homes.

*T*he laity . . . are called to . . . interior
spiritual growth, which makes them
fellow workers of the Holy Spirit.
With his gifts, he renews, rejuvenates
and perfects the work of Christ.

Inasmuch as [man] is an incarnate spirit,
that is, a soul expressing itself in the body,
a body informed by an immortal spirit, man
is called to love in this his unified totality.

*T*rusting in the power of this same Holy Spirit, we pledge ourselves anew to work . . . with firm faith, renewed Hope, and ever deeper Love.

This love of God has appeared over us
in the person of the Holy Spirit,
the spirit of truth.
. . . Love grows through truth;
truth reaches men through love.

Relating

to

Others

*In the name of God: respect, protect, love and serve life,
every human life! Only in this direction will you find justice,
development, true freedom, peace and happiness.*[7]

*A*ccept the great truth on man. Accept this dimension of man, which has opened to all mankind. . . . Accept the mystery in which everyone lives since Christ was born. . . . God was pleased with man through Christ.

Man . . .
it is not permissible
to humiliate him;
it is not permitted
to hate him.

*J*esus was to be invited by men and women
many more times during the course
of his teaching activity. He would accept
their invitations. He would relate to them,
sit down at table and talk.

*J*esus Christ *can be contemporaneously*
the Guest of all persons and all communities
inviting Him, in a new way, that is,
a sacramental and mystical way.

*C*hristians ought to rise together
in defense of spiritual and moral values
against the pressure of materialism
and moral permissiveness.

"Should anyone ask you the reason for this hope of yours, be ever ready to reply, but speak gently and respectfully. Keep your conscience clear" (1 Pt 3:15–16). These words are the golden rule for relationships and contacts which the Christian has to have with his fellow citizen of a different faith.

Our God is a God of compassion and consolation. And he expects us to take the ordinary means to prevent, relieve and remove suffering and sickness.

I also know personally what it means to be sick and to stay in the hospital for a long time, and how it is possible to comfort and support others who share the same lot of confinement and suffering, and how necessary it is to pray for the sick and to show them one's loving concern.

$\mathcal{Y}$ou especially who are tried by sickness,

please unite the oblation of your sufferings

and follow me closely in that

way during my journeys.

You can do much for me.

*T*o tell the truth, we do not find this word "love" (*God is love*) in the story of creation. However, the story often repeats "God saw how good it was." We are led through these words to see love as the divine motivation of creation, almost the source from which it flowed: in fact *only love gives rise to good and delights in the good* (1 Cor 13).

*I*s there not need for . . . generous and disinterested service in our day? Even when there are no hungry in the material sense, how many feel alone and abandoned, sad and desperate, without the warmth of sincere affection and the light of an ideal which is not deceptive? . . . Who will bring them peace and joy, a smile and hope?

A time [of truth] . . . makes us think
about our relations with "Our Father."
It is a time which reestablishes the order that
ought to reign among brothers and sisters. . . .
"I give you a new commandment:
love one another" (Jn 13:34).

The Good Samaritan is each of us!
Through vocation! Through duty!
The Good Samaritan lives charity.
St. Paul says, "This makes us
ambassadors for Christ"
(2 Cor 5:20).

God's grace is possible]
through practice of authentic charity,
which should let shine out all that love of which
the Lord has already made us the object.

*L*et us be ready to let ourselves be
enriched by the grace of the Resurrection by
freeing ourselves from every false treasure. Those
material goods which are often not necessary to
us, for millions of human beings constitute
the essential conditions for survival.

*T*urning to God through prayer
goes along with turning to mankind.
By being demanding with ourselves
and generous with others,
we give expression to our conversion
in both a concrete and a social way.

*T*hrough fuller solidarity with mankind,
with the suffering and especially with the needy,
we unite with Christ, suffering and crucified.

The second commandment is like the first (cf. Mt 22:39) and forms one whole with it. We must love others with the same love which God pours into our hearts and with which he himself loves us. Here, too, what obstacles stand in the way of making the other our neighbor: we do not love God and our brethren enough.

Our relationships with our neighbor
are of capital importance. And when I say
"neighbor," I obviously mean those who live
beside us, in the family, in the neighborhood,
in the town or village, in the city.

"Neighbor"] also means those with whom we work, those who are suffering, are sick, know loneliness, are really poor.

*S*haring is a duty which no one of goodwill,

above all no disciple of Christ, can evade.

Christ requires an opening toward others from me. But toward what other? Toward the one who is by me, at this moment! This call of Christ's cannot be "put off" till an indefinite future when the "right" beggar will appear and put out his hand.

The charity of good example is above all most pleasing to the Lord. Good example is required by the fact that we belong to a family of faithful whose members are independent; each needs help and support from the others.

*M*orality and law are the fundamental conditions for social order. States and nations are built upon law, without which they perish.

*L*et all the communities of the People of God, from the rising of the sun even to its going down, join together. . . . Let all men of goodwill be with us! This is indeed the day that the Lord has made!

*T*he victory of life, the victory of good over evil. It is from this Christian certainty of the victory over every fear of death that your march toward a juster and more human future should take its steps: a future of liberty for God's children.

*D*efend with force the dignity and the rights of every man against the oppressions and vexations of the powerful. . . . Set oneself to true reconciliation among men and Christians.

*O*nly after we have had such "transformation" through the power of truth itself, and of love, should *transformation of the world* be attempted. This is a process beginning from the personal dimension and going toward the community dimension.

Christian values: loyalty to proverbial honesty, fidelity to pledges undertaken and the given word, the sacredness of the family, hard working and generosity toward the poor. These all objectively make up a precious heritage.

*L*et us not call the demands of truth,

conscience and dignity a purely "political" choice.

Those are supreme demands; therefore man

may not renounce them.

*W*e each form a part of God's overall plan. *An exclusively personal and private attitude to salvation is not Christian* and is born of a fundamentally mistaken mentality.

Your lives cannot be lived in isolation, and even *in deciding your future you must always keep in mind your responsibility* as a Christian toward others.

*B*e active members of the People of God; be reconciled with each other and devoted to the work of justice, which will bring peace on earth.

The message we preach is not the wisdom of this world but *the words of life* that seem like foolishness to the unspiritual man.

When we are shaken by the sight of evil spreading in the universe, with all the devastation which it produces, we should not forget that such unleashing of the forces of sin is overcome by the saving power of Christ.

Spirituality
of
Work

Call to holiness. . . . This vocation is universal and concerns
each of the baptized, every Christian. It is always very personal,
connected to work, to one's profession. It is an account
rendered of the talents each person has received—whether
one has made good or bad use of them.[8]

The world entrusted by the Creator
to man as a task always and everywhere on
earth and in every society and nation is
"the world of work."
"World of work" means at the same time
"human world."

New communications techniques will help greater sharing in events and an increased exchange of ideas.

$\mathcal{L}$ove . . . the truth,

by dedicating yourselves carefully

to the work of your perfection.

*A*t the level of knowledge and experience, you shall be *truly competent in your specific field,* so as to exercise, through your presence, this apostolate of testimony and engagement toward others which your consecration and your life in the Church impose on you.

The Christian vocation is essentially apostolic.
Only in this dimension of service to the Gospel
will the Christian find the fullness of
his dignity and responsibility.

*M*an actually knows how to surpass himself infinitely. Evident proof of this is to be seen in the efforts which so many creative geniuses make in order to incarnate transcendental values of beauty and truth lastingly in works of art and thought, values which are more or less momentarily perceived as expressions of the absolute.

Relating
to
God

Life, especially human life, belongs only to God: for this reason whoever attacks human life in some way attacks God himself.[9]

God's salvation is the work of a love greater than man's sin. . . . Love alone can consolidate man in the good; in the unalterable and eternal good.

*T*ruth, like Jesus Christ,

may always be denied,

persecuted, combatted, wounded,

martyred, crucified;

but it always lives again and rises again

and cannot be wrenched out of

the human heart.

Christ, look down upon us;
see the desire of so many hearts!
You who are Lord of history and
Lord of human hearts, be with us!
Jesus Christ, eternal Son of God,
be with us!

*J*esus Himself is given to us and is assigned as a task to the child's soul because, through Jesus, and only by virtue of Him, the Kingdom of God makes a beginning in man and develops.

And how much man loses when he does not see his own humanity in Him. Christ actually came into the world so as to reveal man fully to man and make his most lofty vocation known to him. "Any who did accept Him, he empowered to become children of God" (Jn 1:12).

Creation is a gift, because man appears in it, and he, as "the image of God," is capable of comprehending the very meaning of the gift in the calling out of nothing into existence. And he is capable of responding to the Creator with the language of this comprehension.

*I*s not the fear which upsets modern man

also something which, *in its deepest roots,*

has arisen from "the death of God"?

Not that death on the cross, . . .

but from the death whereby man makes

God die in himself, particularly in the course

of the last stage of his story, in his thought,

in his conscience, in his workings.

Of what use are entire philosophical systems,

social, economic and political programs?

We live . . . in an epoch of gigantic material

progress, which is also the epoch of a negation

of God previously unknown. Such is the

image of our society.

The great tragedy of history

is that Jesus is not known,

is consequently not loved, not followed.

You know Christ!

You know who He is!

Yours is a great privilege!

Know how to be always

worthy and conscious of it!

"I believe in God, Father Almighty, Creator of Heaven and Earth."
This is *the first truth of the faith*,
the first article of our Creed.
Creatures give testimony
of God the Creator.

We ought to be men and women of faith, like Abraham; men and women, that is, who do not count so much on themselves as on the word, the grace and the power of God. The Lord Jesus, while living on earth, personally revealed this way to His disciples.

We must live in intimacy with Him, open up our hearts to Him, our consciences; . . . grace ought to be "over us." . . . Hence it is necessary for us simply to open up to it.

$\mathcal{B}$eing free means achieving
the fruits of liberty, acting in the truth.
Being free also means knowing how to yield,
how to submit to the truth, not to subject truth
to oneself, to one's fancies and will, to one's
interests at the present time.

*I*f it is true that sin in a certain sense shuts man off from God, it is likewise true that *remorse* for sins opens up all the greatness and majesty of God, his fatherhood above all, to man's conscience.

*M*an remains shut to God so long as the words "Father, I have sinned against you" are absent from his lips, above all while they are absent from his *conscience*, from his "*heart.*"

Christ is the Alpha and Omega,
the beginning and the end of everything.
All times and ages belong to Him.
To Him be glory forevermore.
May the light of Christ,
the light of the faith, continue to shine. . . .
May no darkness ever extinguish it!

On the Day of the Resurrection the truth of Christ's words was confirmed, the Truth that the Kingdom of God has come to us, the Truth of the whole of His messianic mission.

The sin in our hearts, the injustices we commit,

the hatred and divisions which we nourish—

all these things cause us not to love God

yet with all our souls, with all our strength. . . .

[Let] the Lord make us his neighbor

and save us with his love.

*S*ince you have been raised up in company with Christ, *set your hearts on what pertains to higher realms* (Col 3:1). . . . That . . . is written in the very structure of man, who loves in the full dimension of his humanity only when he is capable of *surpassing himself with the power of truth and love.*

So we . . . must address ourselves to the Lord Jesus with the readiness of lively faith, with the force of ardent love.

*I*n the language of the Bible,

the heart signifies man's *spiritual inner part*,

it particularly means the *conscience*.

*I*f you are good, responsive,

dedicated to the well-being of others,

loyal servants of the Gospel, then Jesus Himself

will be giving that good impression;

but if you should be weak and unspirited,

then you will be casting a shadow

over His real identity,

and you will not be honoring Him.

All those who receive the word of the Gospel,
all those who nourish themselves on the
Body and Blood of Christ in the Eucharist
under the breath of the Spirit, profess:
"Jesus is Lord" (1 Cor 12:3).

*H*ow important it is, then, for the faithful, as they take part in the Eucharist, to assume a personal attitude of offering. It is not sufficient that they listen to the word of God, nor that they pray in common. It is necessary for them to make Christ's oblation their own, offering up their pains, their difficulties, their trials and, even more, themselves, together with Him and in Him so as to make this gift rise even to the Father, with the gift which Christ makes of Himself.

*W*e must not tamper with God's word. We must strive to apply the Good News to the ever-changing conditions of the world but, courageously and at all costs, we must resist the temptation to alter its content or reinterpret it in order to make it fit the spirit of the present age.

The mystery of Christ,

the Son of God made man,

illuminated the profoundest aspects

of human existence, definitively,

with His Death and His Resurrection.

The mystery of man—

in the insuperable tension

between his finiteness

and his yearning for the infinite,

man bears within himself an

unrenounceable question of the

ultimate meaning of life.

*I*nasmuch as we are witnesses to God,
we are not proprietors who can do what we like
with the announcement received.
We are responsible for a gift which
must be faithfully transmitted.

The education and the training of the conscience in the spirit of justice proceed, together with individual initiatives especially within the apostolate of the laity continuing to develop in that spirit.

*S*cientific culture today requires
Christians to have a mature faith,
an openness toward the language
and to the questions of the learned,
a sense of the orders of knowledge and
of differing approaches to truth.

*A*s Christians, we believe that the ultimate meaning of life and its fundamental values are indeed revealed in Jesus Christ. It is He—Jesus Christ, true God and true man— who says to you, "You address me as 'Teacher' and 'Lord,' and fittingly enough, for that is what I am" (Jn 13:13).

*E*ver fresh souls . . .

unite their sufferings with

Christ's sacrifice, in a joint "offertory,"

which surpasses time and space

and embraces the whole of mankind

and saves it.

Lumen ad revelationem gentium—

a revealing light to the Gentiles.

Death on the cross did not put out Christ's light.

He was not crushed by the tomb slab. . . .

So, we enter . . . bearing light,

the sign of Christ crucified and risen again.

*T*he divine bounty
wishes to be visible today . . .
present through our love.

*L*et us not forget
that God's love for his people,
Christ's love for the Church,
is everlasting and can
never be broken.

Notes

(Except for the sources indicated below, all quotations are from *Prayers and Devotions from Pope John Paul II* [New York: Viking Penguin, 1994].)

1. John Paul II, Encyclical Letter. *The Gospel of Life* (Boston: Pauline Books and Media, 1995), 15.
2. Ibid.
3. Ibid., 16.
4. Ibid., 18.
5. John Paul II, Address to youth rally, New York, October 1995.
6. John Paul II, *Crossing the Threshold of Hope* (New York: Alfred A. Knopf, 1994), 94.
7. John Paul II, *Gospel*, 17.
8. John Paul II, *Crossing*, 180.
9. John Paul II, *Gospel*, 23.